ON THE TRAIL OF
THE

ROMANS
IN BRITAIN

RICHARD WOOD

W

FR   S

© 1999 Franklin Watts
First published in Great Britain by
Franklin Watts
96 Leonard Street
London EC2A 4XD

Franklin Watts Australia
14 Mars Road
Lane Cove
NSW 2006
Australia

ISBN 0 7496 3226 7 (hbk)
ISBN 0 7496 3818 4 (pbk)

Dewey Decimal Classification: 941.01
A CIP record for this book is available
from the British Library

Printed at Oriental Press, Dubai, U.A.E.

Planning and production by Discovery Books Ltd
Editor: Helena Attlee
Designer: Simon Borrough
Consultant: Tim Copeland
Art: Mike Lacey, Stuart Carter, Stefan Chabluk

Photographs: All photographs by Alex Ramsay
except for: British Museum: page 4;
Bristol Museums (courtesy of
The Lydney Park Estate): page 13;
Colchester Museums: pages 5, 17;
Corinium Museum, Cirencester: 23 top, 24;
English Heritage: pages 20, 21;
Museum of London: page 12;
Newcastle Museum of Antiquities: page 15;
Shrewsbury Museum Service: page 11.

CONTENTS

ROMAN INVASION

In the spring of AD 43, about 50,000 Roman soldiers landed on the south coast of Britain.

This vast army marched up through Kent. When the soldiers reached the River Medway the Britons did everything they could to stop them. There was a long and bloody battle which the well-trained Roman troops won.

In August that year, the Roman emperor Claudius arrived, bringing a troop of elephants with him. He knew that the Britons would never have seen any animals so large or so frightening.

The army proceeded north, with Claudius at its head. They took the city of Colchester and made it their capital. Over the next 35 years, they conquered the country to the north as far as the Scottish Highlands.

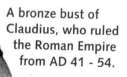

A bronze bust of Claudius, who ruled the Roman Empire from AD 41 - 54.

◀ **The Roman Empire at its largest, during the reign of the Emperor Hadrian, between AD 117 and AD 138.**

Britain was now a part of the Roman Empire. The Britons used the same coins, travelled on the same kinds of roads and wore similar clothes to everyone else in the Empire - even those as far away as North Africa and the Middle East.

TUNICS AND TOGAS

Many of the Britons began to dress like Romans. They wore tunics and thick cloaks to keep them warm. We know that the women loved jewellery because many brooches and bracelets from this period have been found. Rich men started wearing the toga. This was a long piece of cloth that was wrapped around the body in lots of complicated folds.

Rich Roman Britons modelled their clothes and hairstyles on the latest fashions from Rome. Sometimes, the only way to find out what the Romans were wearing in Rome was to look at the pictures on coins.

◀ This beautiful bracelet was found in Colchester, the capital city of Roman Britain.

Very few Romans from Italy ever lived in Britain but the Britons copied the Roman way of life.

The things that the Romans left behind help us to understand how they lived. Archaeologists are like detectives, examining clues in the soil to learn more about life long ago. This book tells you what they have discovered by studying the places where the Roman Britons lived and worked.

A ROMAN ROAD

The Romans' well-organized way of life would have been impossible without good roads.

In less than a century, 16,000 km (10,000 miles) of new roads were built in Britain.

The new roads connected towns, forts and farms, allowing people and goods to travel quickly and safely all over the country. At Blackstone Edge in Lancashire, you can still walk on the actual stones that the Romans laid down 2,000 years ago.

▼ The Roman road at Blackstone Edge. On the steepest sections of the road a deep channel has been worn down its centre. This was made by the poles that were attached to carts and used as brakes.

THE ROMAN POSTAL SYSTEM

Roman roads were so good that the Emperor Augustus was able to set up the world's first efficient postal system. Messengers carried letters, news and military orders right across the Empire. They changed horses at post houses every 15 Roman miles (13 modern miles or 20km), and stayed overnight at inns called *mansiones*. Milestones were set up at regular intervals to help them to find their way. This one at Chesterholm near Hadrian's Wall is two metres tall and still in its original position.

◀ The large, carefully-selected cobble-stones that were put in place by the Romans to create the surface of the road can still be seen today.

Some of our main roads follow the line of ancient Roman roads such as the Fosse Way (the A46 from Exeter to Lincoln).

By excavating Blackstone Edge, archaeologists have been able to find out how the Romans built their roads.

First they dug parallel ditches nine metres apart to mark the edges of the road. Earth and rubble were piled between the ditches to make a low mound called the *agger*. Into this they dug a trench to make the road, filling it with large stones at the bottom and smaller ones above.

At Blackstone Edge, they surfaced the road with blocks of smooth stone which fitted tightly together like a jigsaw. Sometimes, roads were finished with gravel.

• Important towns

N

Stanegate

Dere St.

Ermine St.

Fosse Way

Watling St.

Stane St.

A ROMAN DEFENCE

Roman soldiers had to be very skilled builders. The army formed a huge workforce that was employed to build roads, bridges and aqueducts.

In AD 122, the Emperor Hadrian told his army to build the largest structure ever made anywhere in the Roman Empire. It was a wall 80 Roman miles (73.5 modern miles or 118 km) long, running from one side of Britain to the other.

Hadrian's Wall was a customs post, controlling the movement of people and trade between England and Scotland. It was part of a system of defences. In front of it there was a very wide, deep ditch and about half a mile behind it was the *vallum*. This was another ditch which ran between two high earth mounds.

If you visit Hadrian's Wall, you can still see the milecastles which were built every Roman mile along its length. These were little forts where small groups of soldiers were stationed.

The Romans said that Hadrian's Wall was built to separate the Romans from the Barbarians! The shorter Antonine Wall was built further north by the Emperor Antoninus Pius, Hadrian's successor.

N

Antonine Wall

Newcastle-upon-Tyne

Bowness-on-Solway   Hadrian's Wall

About 9,500 soldiers were needed on the Wall. Most of them were housed in 15 forts which could accommodate hundreds of men. There were store rooms, baths and dormitories in the forts, as well as a comfortable, private house for the commander.

Letters written by Roman soldiers serving on the Wall have survived. They tell us that it was a cold and lonely life. Many of the troops longed to go home to France or Italy.

The Wall took 15 years and two million tonnes of stone to complete. The soldiers did their job so well that much of Hadrian's Wall still stands today.

ROMAN CONVENIENCE

These are the soldiers' lavatories at Housesteads Fort on Hadrian's Wall. There was seating for 16 and running water for dipping the sponges they used instead of paper.

A ROMAN TOWN

York, Leicester and many other British cities are built on top of Roman towns. When land is dug up to make way for new buildings or roads ancient remains are often found.

In Wroxeter, the town known as Viroconium to the Romans, archaeologists have uncovered some inscriptions. These carved messages tell us that in AD 130 the Emperor Hadrian gave orders for the town to be enlarged and given a grand new forum, or market place. Viroconium soon became the capital of the whole region and the fourth largest town in Britain. After the Romans left Britain, Wroxeter was abandoned. Very few modern buildings have ever been built there.

The 'Old Work' is the name given to the large piece of Roman wall that originally separated the baths from the exercise hall.

FIRE IN THE FORUM

One market day 1,800 years ago, fire broke out in the forum at Viroconium. Archaeologists have used the remains to piece together a picture of the event. They can tell that the traders escaped, but they had no time to pack up their wares. These have been found buried under the remains of the arcade roof. When fire broke out, one trader abandoned 200 valuable

Samian ware bowls from France. Another left a crate of mixing bowls and an ironmonger lost 100 whetstones, used for sharpening tools.

Major Roman towns in Britain.

N

Carlisle • Corbridge

Aldborough • York

Chester • Lincoln

Caistor •by· Norwich

Wroxeter • Leicester

Gloucester St.Albans Colchester
Caerleon• Cirencester • London
Caerwent Bath Silchester Canterbury
  • Chichester
Exeter• Dorchester

In the town centre of Viroconium archaeologists discovered the bases of 16 columns. The evidence suggests that they once supported the roof of a covered arcade surrounding the forum. You can also see the foundations of a huge public bath house. The remains of a furnace tell us that the Romans heated their water and their rooms, just as we do.

The remains of the furnace used for heating water and providing underfloor heating.

A ROMAN PORT

Rich Roman Britons bought delicate glassware from Germany, Samian ware pottery from France, oil from Spain and spices from the Middle East.

These luxury goods had to be brought to Britain by sea. London was only a day's sail from the Continent. A network of roads fanned out from the city in every direction. London soon became the entry point for many of the luxury goods imported into Roman Britain.

▼ Roman quays and warehouses stood along the banks of the Thames in London. This model is based on the evidence found by archaeologists.

Evidence discovered on the banks of the Thames tells us what goods were imported. For example, Samian ware pottery looking as good as new has been discovered in the soft mud. It must have been accidentally dropped overboard 1,800 years ago.

Two Roman shipwrecks have been located in the Thames. One, found near the old County Hall, was of an ocean-going boat which would have crossed the Channel and come up the Thames on the tide. The other, a barge which was probably used for coastal trading. It was found with a cargo of building stone on board.

Roman ports in Britain.

FOREIGN TRADE

This is a bronze figure of a deerhound, the kind of dog that was probably exported to the Continent.

Roman documents have survived to this day which tell us that the Britons exported many goods. Tin from Cornwall, lead from Northumberland and gold from Wales all went overseas. So did oysters, corn, baskets, woollen clothes and even hunting dogs.

Some British products have messages written on them. In Dover, a tile has been discovered with the words 'I made 550 tiles' scrawled across it. Someone else had added another message which said: 'And I smashed 51 of them' underneath!

13

A ROMAN TEMPLE

The Romans were pagans who worshipped many different gods. The god Mithras was popular among soldiers. Temples to Mithras were always the same shape.

Archaeologists have excavated these remains of the temple at Carrawburgh.

At Carrawburgh, which is close to Hadrian's Wall, archaeologists found the temple walls, three small altars and the remains of stone seats.

We know that a meal was eaten during the worship of Mithras. Chicken bones have been discovered at Carrawburgh. They may have been thrown away at the end of the ceremony.

Candle-holders, incense burners and scented pine cones have also been discovered. These clues help us to imagine what the temple was like - dark, mysterious, and scented with sweet-smelling smoke.

Near to the entrance there is a deep pit, where men were buried alive. They were then 'reborn' as true followers of Mithras.

The three altars at Carrawburgh Temple, where worshippers once offered gifts of food to the god Mithras.

The temple at Carrawburgh was probably abandoned when the locals became Christians. At first the authorities did not like Christians because they refused to worship the Emperor. However, in AD 313 the Emperor Constantine allowed Christians to practise their religion. Pictures of Christ or the Greek letters Chi-Ro (meaning Christ) can sometimes be found on mosaics, wall paintings or silver dishes.

In the Newcastle Museum of Antiquities you can visit a full-sized model of the Carrawburgh temple as it originally looked.

ROMAN THEATRES

The Romans believed that they had to live in a town, with its shops, baths and temples, in order to enjoy a civilized life.

A Roman writer called Tacitus tells us that St Albans, known as Verulamium, was a *municipium*. This was the name given to an important place. It had several shops, spacious baths and stone-built temples. The remains of these buildings can all be seen today.

Verulamium also had a theatre which stood conveniently close to the centre of the town. The remains of nearby ruins have been studied by archaeologists who believe that the audience would have passed public toilets and shops selling snacks on their way to the theatre.

The surviving stone walls and earth banks of the Roman theatre at St Albans.

On reaching the theatre, the people climbed up wooden steps on the outside of the walls.

A theatre building in Canterbury had a massive stone outer wall, part of which still survives. In St Albans there are steep earth banks on which tiers of wooden seats were arranged. Roman writings tell us that the stage was covered. By studying the ruins, archaeologists have found that it was designed with a curtain that could be lowered in front of it. Up to 2,000 people could be packed in to see the play. They sat in the open air.

key
ⅿ Theatre
◎ Amphitheatre

N

Deva (Chester)

Isca (Caerleon)

Verulamium (St. Albans)

Corinium (Cirencester)

Calleva (Silchester)

Durovernum Cantiacorum (Canterbury)

Durnovaria (Dorchester)

The remains of theatres and amphitheatres have been excavated in towns all over the south of England.

FIGHT TO THE DEATH

Most Roman towns also had an amphitheatre. This was like a large, oval football stadium, normally just outside the town. Many amphitheatre shows were horribly cruel. Men boxed with iron-studded gloves, slaves and prisoners were savaged by wild animals, and gladiators fought to the death with swords and nets.

This pottery vase from Colchester is decorated with pictures of gladiators fighting.

17

ROMAN BATHS

In Britain today, most of us take regular baths. So did the Roman Britons, but instead of bathing at home, many people went to public baths.

▶ The site of the Sulis Spring in Bath. The goddess Sulis was also known by the Roman name of Minerva.

In Bath, which is in Somerset, you can still see parts of one of the largest Roman baths in Europe. Bath was a very special place. It was called Aquae Sulis ('Waters of Sulis') after Sulis, the ancient British deity associated with healing.

Warm water still gushes out of the ground in Bath today. The Romans thought that drinking or bathing in this water could heal all sorts of illnesses. They believed that the water was a gift from Sulis and they built a grand temple in her honour.

For Roman Britons, the Great Bath was the star attraction. They used it for swimming as well as the serious business of keeping clean.

The Romans did not use soap to keep themselves clean. Instead they took a hot bath and then they rubbed oil all over their bodies. The oil was scraped off by slaves who used a scraper called a strigil for the job. As the oil came off, so did all the dirt, leaving the body feeling very clean and fresh. Look out for a strigil in the archaeology displays of your local museum.

N

Chesters

Wall
Wroxeter ⊟ ⊟ ⊟ Leicester

⊟ ⊟ Silchester
Bath

Roman bath towns

The Great Bath is filled with warm spring water which steams in cold weather. The pool was lined with lead to prevent leaks.

You can still follow in the footsteps of Roman bathers. First they took off their clothes in the *apodyterium*. Then they passed though the *frigidarium* or cold room to the smaller warm and hot baths (*tepidarium* and *caldarium*).

A ROMAN VILLA

For part of the year rich Roman families left town to enjoy the peace of the countryside. They built luxurious country houses called villas.

This mosaic floor at Lullingstone shows the goddess Europa being captured by Jupiter, who is disguised as a bull.

The owners of Lullingstone Villa in Kent must have led a fine life. Their home overlooked the river. It was heated and decorated with beautiful mosaic floors in all of the main rooms. Some people believe that the owners of Lullingstone were not Britons. Statues have been found there that look as though they were made in Eastern Europe. They may have been portraits of the owner's family overseas.

Today, you can see the layout of the main villa building at Lullingstone. The largest room was the *triclinium* (dining room), where the owner entertained guests. The huge mosaic floor remains, with pictures of heroes like Bellerophon, riding the winged horse Pegasus. You can imagine where the guests sat, on three couches arranged around the pictures on the floor.

A detail from the Europa mosaic.

In recent years, the sites of many more Roman villas have been spotted from the air. In very dry weather, marks sometimes appear in the crops where buildings once stood.

Most Roman villas were in the south of England, though remains have been found as far north as Yorkshire. The map shows important villas which can be visited.

N

Chedworth
Lullingstone
Bignor
Rockbourne
Fishbourne
Brading

Above a wall, for example, the soil is thin and it dries out quickly in hot weather. Plants growing in this spot can become unhealthy or even die off.

Where there were ditches or trenches, on the other hand, the soil stays moist and the plants are a healthy, dark green. Viewed from an aeroplane, these differences in colour can show up the outlines of long-lost roads, fields and houses.

21

ROMAN COUNTRYSIDE

Rich Romans built fine houses in the British countryside. They increased their wealth by growing crops and keeping animals to sell in nearby towns.

Chedworth Villa today. The remains of the walls are clearly visible, but the rooms with mosaics are protected by modern buildings.

Chedworth in Gloucestershire is in a beautiful valley close to the important Roman town of Corinium, which is also in Gloucestershire, and is now called Cirencester. The spacious rooms and splendid decoration of the villa show what a comfortable life the owners must have enjoyed.

The main buildings surround two courtyards. There are two dining rooms, two baths and a number of other rooms whose use we are not sure of. No farm buildings have been found at Chedworth yet, but bones found nearby show that Roman farmers kept the same animals as we do today. There were certainly sheep

FARM TOOLS

One of the mosaics at Chedworth depicts the four seasons. This woman represents summer. She has a sickle in her hand. Roman farm tools have been found near Chedworth. They look very similar to the tools that were used on British farms until Victorian times.

▲ Archaeologists are still working at Chedworth, uncovering further evidence about its use in Roman times.

around Chedworth. Their wool was used to make *birri Britannici* - thick coats which were exported all over Europe.

Wheat was an important crop in Roman Britain. It was ground up to make flour. Thousands of loaves were needed each day to feed the Roman army. Before the Roman invasion, the Britons ate very few types of vegetables. Thanks to the Romans, they found out about carrots, turnips, cabbage, lettuce and onions. Roman farmers also planted grapevines and fig, walnut and sweet chestnut trees.

ROMAN MEALS

Many of the foods that the Roman Britons liked to eat were imported from other parts of the Empire.

The Roman kitchen that has been reconstructed at the Corinium Museum in Cirencester. All of the pots and kitchen equipment were found nearby.

Archaeologists can often guess what different rooms were used for. Mosaic floors were laid in the best rooms, while plain tiles tell us that we might be in a kitchen or a store.

Other things are sometimes discovered that provide clues about the lives of the Romans. In the Corinium Museum in Cirencester they have used these discoveries to reconstruct a Roman kitchen. It is equipped with Roman cooking utensils found in the town. These finds revealed that Roman cooks worked over a charcoal stove raised up on a brick platform, rather like a barbecue. They had iron and bronze frying pans and pots for warming food on an iron grid placed over the fire.

The big pot propped against the stove is an *amphora*. It was

Garlic

Thyme

STRONG TASTES

Parsley, sage, thyme and garlic are all common ingredients in cooking today. Until Roman times, they were unknown in Britain. The Romans liked strong flavours. This may have been because they suffered from mild lead poisoning. The poisoning, which was caused by drinking water carried by lead pipes, would have damaged their sense of taste.

Parsley

Sage

▶ In this full-sized model of a Roman dining room, the diner's couch is placed next to a low table.

used for bringing wine, olive oil and sauces to Britain from the Continent. The Romans were very fond of a special sauce from Spain called liquamen. It was made from rotting fish and had a very sharp flavour. We know that this was used in sweet dishes as well as savoury ones.

A ROMAN GARDEN

By searching the soil for seeds, pollen, or the remains of plants, archaeologists can find out about the gardens laid out around Roman villas.

When Fishbourne in Sussex was excavated, archaeologists discovered a series of trenches filled with dark, rich soil. Soon they realised that these were the beds where hedges and plants had grown. They had discovered the traces of a Roman garden. By piecing together the evidence, it has been possible to replant the site just as it was in about AD 70.

▲ This stone gutter is part of the original, Roman garden. It ran between the wall of the villa and the garden. In the foreground, you can see the base of a pillar and the bottom of a stone tank.

▶ By planting hedges in the original, Roman trenches, archaeologists have been able to recreate the Roman Garden.

The villa at Fishbourne is surrounded by the first known garden ever to be built in Roman Britain. It is very like gardens in other parts of the Empire. It is possible that the rich villa owner paid for a designer and a team of workmen to come to Britain from the Continent.

The Roman garden was an outdoor sitting room. It was a place to meet friends, talk and take exercise. At Fishbourne, a beautiful colonnade enclosed the site. A path wide enough for two people cut across the garden, connecting the entrance hall to the 'audience chamber' where important visitors were received. Hedges on either side of the path created private niches for benches. Elsewhere in the garden, the remains of statues, water pipes and fountains have been found.

Town houses in Roman Britain often had small courtyard gardens. Archaeologists at the museum in Cirencester have recreated the kind of garden that would have been found at Corinium 1,800 years ago.

UNDER ATTACK

For 400 years, the Britons obeyed their Roman rulers. The country was well-organized and peaceful, thanks to the powerful army.

This fort is called Burgh Castle. Jutting out from its walls are round towers called bastions. These held ballistae which were huge catapults for firing stone balls at attackers.

In AD 300, things began to go wrong. Abroad, there were arguments over who should rule the Empire. At home, raiders and pirates from across the seas began to attack Britain.

Saxons and Jutes from Germany and Denmark were the greatest danger. The Romans built a string of 10 forts on the east coast to keep the attackers out. They are called the Saxon Shore Forts, and you can still see most of them today.

The fort at Burgh Castle in Norfolk was known as Gariannonum. Its walls are still nearly three metres thick at the base and five metres high.

N

Brancaster
Burgh Castle

Walton Castle
Bradwell Reculver
Richborough Dover
Portchester Lympne
Pevensey

The Romans built forts in places that they thought were vulnerable to attack.

Stand at Burgh Castle and you can see why the Romans chose this spot. With a wide view across the river estuary and sea, it was an ideal point to defend eastern Britain.

Even the forts could not save Britain. All over the Empire, Roman rule was breaking down. The army in Britain became smaller and smaller. When Rome itself was attacked in AD 410, the Emperor Honorius told the cities of Britain that they had to look after their own defence.

For a time, life went on as before, but by AD 450, Saxon invaders controlled most of the country. Although Roman ways were soon forgotten, they were not completely lost. Following the trail of the Romans is still possible, thanks to the evidence they left behind.

GLOSSARY

aqueduct
a kind of bridge used to carry water above ground level to places where it is needed

arcade
a covered walkway, usually with open arches on one side

Barbarians
wild, uncivilised people

column
stone pillars which support an upper storey of a building or its roof

customs
an office staffed by soldiers who would question the people crossing boundaries between different countries

deity
god or goddess

dormitory
room containing several beds

Emperor
the ruler of all the countries in the Roman Empire

estuary
the place where a river flows into the sea

excavate
dig up soil to search for historic remains

export
send goods to other countries to be sold

forum
the square at the centre of a Roman town that was used as a market place

furnace
a closed fireplace or stove, used for heating water

gladiator
a man who entertained an audience by fighting and killing animals or people

mosaic
a pattern made out of tiny coloured stones

sickle
curved blade with a short handle used for cutting corn

spices
strongly-scented seeds or powders used in small quantities to flavour food

toga
the costume of rich Roman men made from a long sheet of cloth, wrapped around the body

TIMELINE

AD43	The Roman army of the Emperor Claudius conquers southern Britain
49	The city of Colchester made into the first capital of Roman Britain
84	Agricola conquers lowlands of Scotland
122	The Emperor Hadrian orders the Roman army to build Hadrian's Wall
139	Antonine Wall built across southern Scotland
163	Antonine Wall abandoned; Hadrian's Wall strengthened
197	London becomes the capital of 'Upper Britain'
212	Emperor Caracalla makes Roman Britons officially 'citizens of Rome'
275	Saxon Shore forts built
306	Constantine is made Emperor while on a visit to York
313	Christianity is allowed throughout the Empire
367	Roman Britain is attacked from the north and east; Hadrian's Wall overrun
400	Hadrian's Wall is finally abandoned
410	The Emperor Honorius calls troops back to Rome and tells Britons to defend themselves
430	Roman money goes out of use in Britain
450	Saxons invade Britain. Most Roman towns abandoned.

PLACES TO VISIT

Of the many interesting Roman sites to visit in Britain, here are some of the main ones.

Brading, Isle of Wight: Roman villa with remarkable mosaics.

Caister St Edmund, Norfolk: Walled Roman town site.

Caerleon, Gwent: Site of important fortress with theatre and baths.

Dover, Kent: Roman lighthouse, 20m high and painted house.

Portchester, Hampshire: Imposing remains of Saxon shore fort.

Richborough, Kent: Invasion landing site with major Saxon shore fort.

Rough Castle, Central Scotland: Best preserved fort on Antonine Wall, with ramparts and ditches.

South Shields, Tyne and Wear: Important fort with museum.

Wall, Staffordshire: Town site with baths and museum.

York, North Yorkshire: Well-preserved remains of buildings.

INDEX